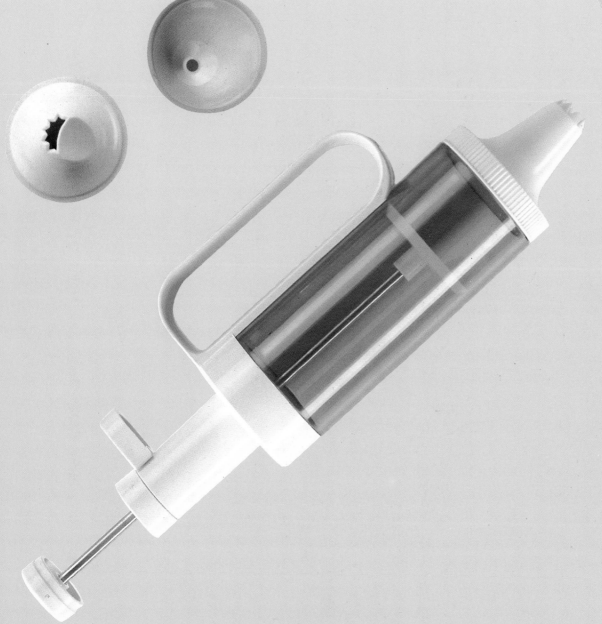

Éclairs & Brown Bears

by Arielle Rosin
photographs by Daniel Czap
research by Etienne Collomb

series under the direction of Caroline Lancrenon

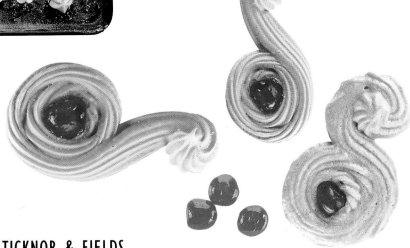

TICKNOR & FIELDS
New York · 1994

CONTENTS

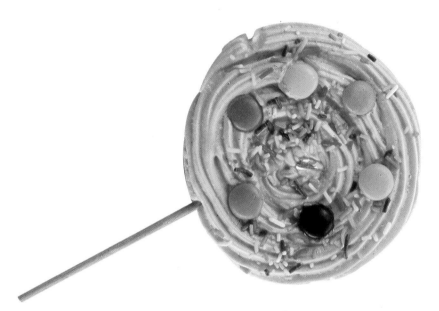

PREFACE

Each chapter of *Eclairs & Brown Bears* first teaches a basic, classic pastry recipe, then offers variations on it. Full instructions are given for the first recipe in each chapter. Additionally, there are some general rules of baking that everyone should know:

• Read a recipe all the way through before starting to make it. Understand all the steps involved. Then put all the equipment and ingredients on the counter or table, ready to be used. The middle of a mixing a cake is not the time to discover that someone has used up all the butter. There are exceptions to this rule: if a recipe requires whipped cream, the cream should be refrigerated until needed because cold cream whips better. But make sure all the ingredients are available.

• Stick to the ingredients listed. Baking is a science as well as an art. A cook can almost always add a little more water to the soup, but only an experienced baker knows the effect extra liquid will have on a cake. Changing the number of eggs or the quantity of water might produce a cake that won't rise. Of course, it is possible to experiment with different flavorings and fillings.

• Measure carefully. If a recipe says "1/2 cup chopped nuts," chop the nuts, then measure them. Use a plastic or metal measuring cup that holds 1/2 cup when filled to the top (not a big glass one—that is for measuring liquids). Cup measurements should be level; spoonfuls should be level, too.

• If a recipe says butter should be room temperature, then leave the butter out of the refrigerator for an hour or so. Don't melt it. The butter should be soft, but not liquid. (Most Americans use salted butter. Classic baking uses unsalted, or "sweet," butter. If it is necessary to use salted butter, leave out any salt that the recipe calls for.)

• To separate an egg, crack the egg carefully—without breaking the yolk—over a small bowl or cup. Hold half the shell in each hand and let the white drip into the cup while pouring the yolk from one half of the shell to the other. Then pour the yolk into a separate dish. When separating many eggs, it is a good idea to separate each one over the cup, then transfer the white to a bigger bowl. Then if one yolk breaks, it will not ruin several egg whites. If there is yolk (or anything oily) mixed with the whites, they will not whip properly.

• Preheat the oven to the temperature called for. Ovens take time to heat, and some pastries will not bake properly unless they are baked right after being made.

• Always place the baking sheet, pie pan, or cake pan in middle to upper third of the oven. When baking cakes or delicate pastries, do not open the oven door until it is time to remove the cake or pastry from the oven.

BROWN BEARS

Utensils
- large mixing bowl
- plastic spatula
- fork
- electric hand mixer
- long metal spatula
- 2 large baking sheets
- cooling rack
- pot holder
- syringe, cookie press, or pastry bag with round 1/4-inch tube
- 2 saucepans or double boiler

Ingredients
(for 20 bears)
- 4 large egg whites
- 2 cups sifted confectioners' sugar
- pat of butter
- small amount of flour
- 6 ounces (6 squares) semisweet chocolate
- candy decorations (icing flowers, silver candy balls)

IMPORTANT:
Bake meringues in dry weather only. Humidity will make them tough and chewy instead of light and crisp.

2

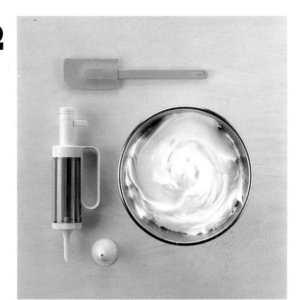

Beat with the electric mixer for about 10 minutes or until the mixture is stiff. Fill the syringe or pastry bag with it, using the plastic spatula.

3

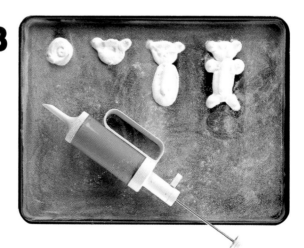

Butter and flour the baking sheets. Draw bear shapes on each sheet with the meringue. Leave at least 2 inches between each bear.

TIP:
To use a pastry bag, fold tube end up to prevent leakage and fill pastry bag with meringue. Then release tube end and twist top of bag to squeeze filling down through the tube.

Preheat the oven to 175° F. Put the egg whites in bowl and add the confectioners' sugar. Place the bowl in a saucepan containing hot (not boiling) water.

4

Bake for about 2 hours or until crisp. Take baking sheets out of the oven with the pot holder. With the metal spatula, remove bears and place on cooling rack. Let them cool for about 30 minutes.

5

While meringues cool, break chocolate into pieces and melt in the top of a double boiler on stove.

DOUBLE BOILER
This consists of a small saucepan resting inside a larger one. Hot water in the lower pan slowly heats the food in the upper one.

6

Using the fork, dip a bear into the melted chocolate, coating it completely. Remove the bear and place it on the rack. Decorate using silver candy balls for the eyes and icing candy flowers for the belt. Repeat for each bear. Let dry for 30 minutes.

Multicolored sprinkles, coconut flakes, and crushed chocolate make good decorations, too. The bears can also be left plain.

LOLLIPOPS

Utensils
- star-shaped tube for pastry bag or syringe

Ingredients
(for 15 lollipops)
- meringue batter (page 9)
- red food coloring
- wooden or rolled paper sticks
- candy decorations (M & M's, flowers, multicolored sprinkles, silver candy balls)

TIP:
Always sift confectioners' sugar before measuring and using in a recipe because it tends to cake together during storage.

Preheat the oven to 175° F. Add a few drops of red food coloring to make the meringue pink. Butter and flour baking sheets. Fill a syringe or pastry bag with meringue and draw 4-inch spirals on cookie sheets. Carefully insert a stick into each. Decorate with sprinkles and other candies. Bake as instructed for the brown bears on page 10.

RINGS

Ingredients (for 20 rings)
- meringue batter (page 9)
- multicolored round sprinkles

Preheat the oven to 175° F. Butter and flour baking sheets. Fill a syringe or pastry bag with meringue, and draw 6-inch rings on cookie sheets. Use star-shaped tube. Decorate rings with sprinkles. Bake as instructed for the brown bears on page 10.

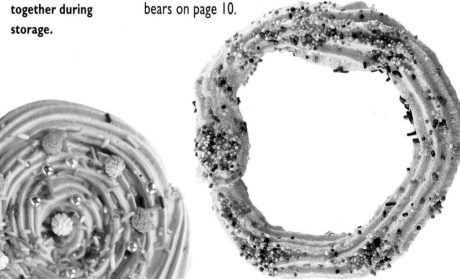

NESTS

Ingredients (for 15 nests)
- uncooked meringue
- 2–3 kiwis
- 3–4 fresh strawberries
- whipped cream

Preheat the oven to 175° F. Butter and flour baking sheets. Fill a syringe or pastry bag with meringue and draw 3-inch spirals on cookie sheets. Use star-shaped tube. Add small meringue flowers around the edges. Bake as instructed for the brown bears on page 10. Peel and slice the kiwis, then cut the slices in half. Wash the strawberries and remove the hulls, then cut them in quarters. Fill the nests with fruit. Top with the whipped cream just before serving.

TIP:
Let meringue nests cool completely before filling, and do not fill with fruit until just before serving or the juices will soften the meringue.

M eringue can be made into swirls, stars, and many other shapes, then decorated with fresh or candied fruit.

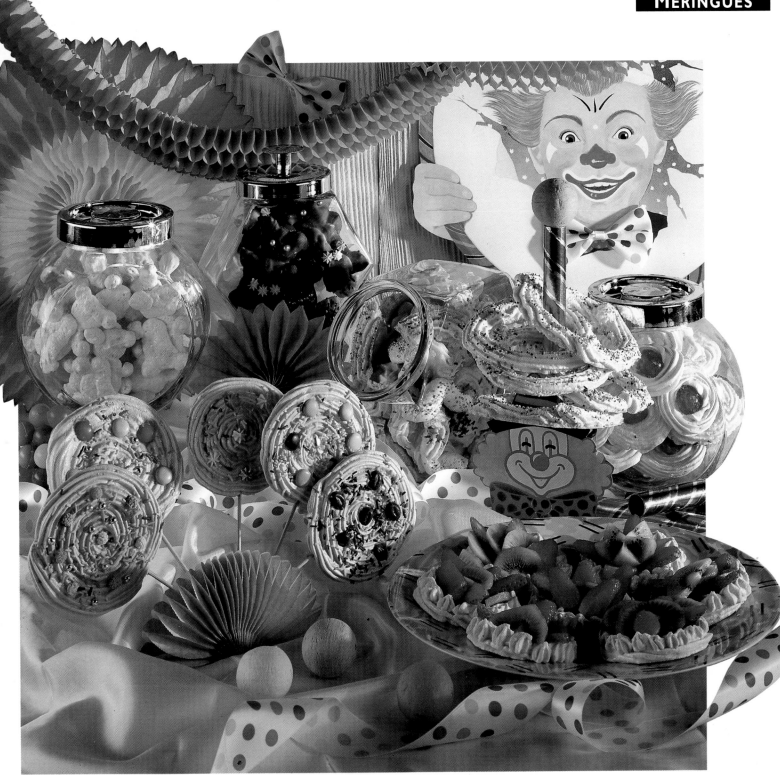

The pastry bag

The pastry bag allows bakers and candy makers to create beautiful decorations from icing or meringue. Invented by a French pastry chef in the late 1700s, a pastry bag can be fitted with different kinds of metal tubes. The shape and diameter of the tube opening determines the pattern that can be made. With a variety of tubes—and much skill—an experienced pastry maker can create complex three-dimensional leaves, flowers, stars, and other designs. Before the invention of the pastry bag, meringues were shaped with a spoon.

The history of meringue

In 1720, Stanislas Leczinski, a former king of Poland, was bored with retirement. As a hobby he started to cook. He became more and more interested in cooking, so he asked a famous pastry chef named Gasparini to help him. The chef conducted numerous experiments, and one of his resulting inventions was meringue, named after Meringen, the town where he was born.

Two kinds of meringue

The crunchy white meringue in the previous recipes and the soft gold-and-white meringue on the top of a lemon meringue pie are made in almost the same way. The main difference is in the baking. Slow baking at a very low temperature dries out the mixture without browning it. Quick baking at a higher temperature browns the meringue but leaves it creamy inside.

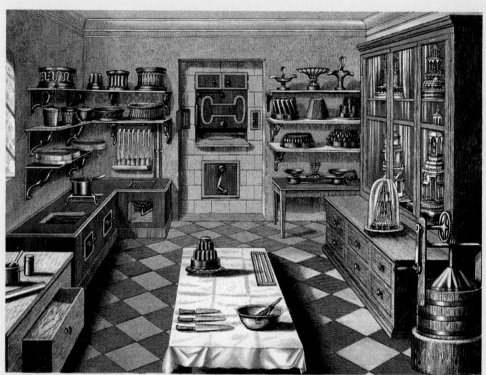

Nineteenth-century France. Illustration from the pastry section of *La Cuisine Artistique* (Artistic Cooking), by Urbain Dubois, Paris, 1882.

During the Renaissance the Italians began making a mixture of egg whites and sugar, although they did not call it meringue. Italian meringue is made with a boiling hot sugar syrup and does not need to be baked.

AN UNUSUAL USE OF MERINGUE

The dessert called "Baked Alaska" is a block of ice cream enclosed in a thin layer of cake and then coated with meringue. When the dessert is baked, the meringue becomes hot and golden brown, but the ice cream does not melt—the meringue insulates it from the heat.

A Chinese cake seller during the Festival of the Moon, held on the fifteenth day of the eighth month of the year. *Cris de Pékin*, about 1785.

Four cake lovers on the attack.

CAKES AND CELEBRATIONS

In many places, birthdays, weddings, and holidays are celebrated with special cakes. Cakes are big enough for a party and can be beautifully decorated. Also, many cakes require ingredients that were once scarce—for instance, refined sugar, white flour, and fresh butter. In years past, these were too expensive for most people to use every day, so they were saved for special occasions.

Traditional cakes differ from place to place. A birthday cake in the United States is often a layer cake or an ice cream cake. In France, the traditional birthday cake is the Gâteau Saint-Honoré, made of cream-puff pastry and custard. In England, it is a fruit cake covered with almond paste and a thick glaze.

BROWNIES WITH M & M'S

Utensils

- 2 saucepans or double boiler
- strainer
- wooden spoon
- large mixing bowl
- whisk
- measuring cup
- 9-inch square cake pan
- teaspoon
- knife

Ingredients

- 4 ounces (4 squares) unsweetened chocolate
- 5 tablespoons unsalted butter
- 1 cup granulated sugar
- 2 large eggs
- 1/2 cup all-purpose flour
- 1 teaspoon vanilla extract
- pinch of salt
- 3/4 cup M & M's

Cut the butter into small pieces. Remove the chocolate from the heat and add the butter. Blend with whisk until butter is melted and mixed with chocolate.

DOUBLE BOILER

This consists of a smaller saucepan resting inside a larger saucepan. Food in the upper pan is heated slowly by the hot water in the lower one, and does not burn.

Preheat the over to 350° F. Melt the chocolate in the top of a double boiler.

Add the sugar and eggs, and mix well.

4

TIP:
While brownies are still warm, lightly cut the surface crust to mark the squares. This will make cutting them easier when they are cool.

Stir the flour, vanilla, and salt into the mixture. Fold in most of the M & M's. Butter the cake pan and pour in the batter and spread evenly in pan. Decorate the top with remaining candies.

5

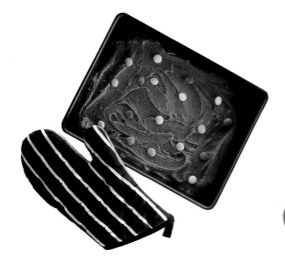

Bake for 25–30 minutes. Use the pot holder to remove the pan from the oven. Cut the brownies into small squares when cool.

WHITE CHOCOLATE BROWNIES WITH ALMONDS

Ingredients
- brownie batter (page 17)
- 3/4 cup ground almonds
- 1/2 cup slivered almonds

- 4 ounces white chocolate

Preheat the oven to 350° F. Prepare the batter as instructed, using white chocolate instead of dark, 3/4 cup of sugar instead of 1 cup, and ground almonds instead of M & M's.

TIP:
Brownies will keep for several days in an airtight container.

Sprinkle the top with almonds and bake as instructed on page 18.

WALNUT BROWNIES

Ingredients
- brownie batter (page 17)
- 1 cup walnut halves

Preheat the oven to 350° F. Prepare the batter as instructed, but chop half the walnuts and use instead of M & M's.

Sprinkle the top with remaining walnut halves and bake as instructed on page 18. These brownies are great served with vanilla ice cream.

HONEY PEANUT BROWNIES

Ingredients
- brownie batter (page 17)
- 1 cup honey-coated peanuts

Preheat the oven to 350° F. Prepare the batter as instructed, chop half the peanuts and use instead of M & M's. Sprinkle the top with the remaining peanuts and bake as instructed on page 18.

COCONUT BROWNIES

Ingredients
- brownie batter (page 17)
- 3/4 cup dried coconut
- 3/4 cup bananas chips

Preheat the oven to 350° F. Prepare the batter as instructed, but use most of the coconut and banana chips instead of M & M's. Sprinkle more coconut and banana chips on the top and bake as instructed on page 18.

Iced brownies make good birthday cakes. Melt 4 ounces (4 squares) semisweet chocolate in a double boiler and spread on top. Let cool and chill to harden, if desired, before serving.

BROWNIES

The French have their crepes, the English their scones, but brownies are a completely American treat. No one is sure how they originated. One story says that they were the result of an accident: a chocolate cake did not rise properly in the oven, resulting in a dense and chewy bar cookie. Instead of arguing about origins, most brownie enthusiasts debate whether the perfect brownie should be cakelike or fudgelike, and whether or not it should be iced.

COOKIES, CRACKERS, AND BISCUITS

Americans have cookies and crackers; the British call the same things biscuits, though in America a biscuit is similar to a British scone. Names can be confusing! The word biscuit comes from the French and means "twice-cooked"—which the first French cookies were. The double cooking removed all the moisture, so the biscuits did not spoil. The American word cookie comes from a Dutch word meaning "little cake."

A BRITISH INDUSTRIAL TRADITION

Great Britain was the first country to mass produce cookies and crackers. In 1815, the Carr Company opened the first baking factory. Other factories soon followed, as Great Britain began exporting its biscuits all over the world. It wasn't long after, that American companies began manufacturing cookies as well. Although Americans buy huge quantities of factory-made cookies and crackers, they also have a tradition of baking cookies at home. In contrast, Europeans are much more likely to buy their baked goods than to make them at home.

AFTERNOON TEA

The English tradition of afternoon tea is believed to have begun in the nineteenth century. At the time, the upper classes ate lunch very early and dinner quite late. Anna, duchess of Bedford, became hungry, so she started having a snack at four or five o'clock, along with the most popular alcohol-free drink in England: tea. She started a fashion that has been followed by the British ever since.

Depending on time and place, afternoon tea consists of sandwiches, scones, cookies, and small cakes. In winter, tea often includes buttered muffins and toast. Of course, at any time of year the meal includes hot tea, almost always served with milk.

TRAVELER'S BISCUIT

Publicity poster for biscuits, about 1890.

Hard bread has been baked for soldiers since ancient times. By the 1600s, a kind of flat cracker called "hardtack" was the staple food for military campaigns, on merchant sailing ships, and on explorations. The crackers were easy to store and could be kept for up to fifty years, but they deserved their name. The hardtack was so hard that sometimes a hungry traveler had to soak in it water before taking a bite. The French called it "stone bread."

Chocolate

When Spanish explorers brought cocoa beans back to Europe from Central and South America in the 1500s, Europeans did the same thing with the chocolate as the Aztecs and Mayans had: they drank it. It was not until the 1800s that chocolate candy became popular, when manufacturers learned to make chocolate bars. The scientific name for the cocoa tree is *Theobroma cacao*, "the food of the gods."

HEART COOKIES

Utensils

- large mixing bowl
- electric hand mixer
- measuring cup
- rolling pin
- pot holder
- small strainer
- metal and plastic knives
- long metal spatula
- small saucepan
- pastry brush
- teaspoon
- wooden spoon
- 1 large and 1 small heart-shaped cookie cutter
- large baking sheet

Ingredients

(for about 20 cookies)
- 1 egg
- 1/2 cup granulated sugar
- pinch of salt
- 2 cups all-purpose flour
- 1/2 cup (1 stick) unsalted butter
  at room temperature
- 3/4 cup confectioners' sugar
- raspberry jam
- apricot preserves

1

Put the egg, granulated sugar, and salt in the bowl. Beat with the electric mixer until frothy.

2

Add the flour and mix with wooden spoon until well blended.

3

Add the butter in small pieces and mix in with the fingertips. Form the dough into a ball, wrap in plastic, and chill in refrigerator for I hour.

4

Preheat the oven to 350° F. Place half the dough on a buttered and floured baking sheet. Press it down with the hands, then roll it out to a thickness of about 1/8 inch.

TIP:
Butter cookies can also be rolled out on a floured counter or pastry board.

5

Cut hearts out of the dough with large cookie cutter. Use smaller cutter to remove a tiny heart shape from half the cookies. Remove excess dough from baking sheet with metal spatula and set aside.

6

Brush tops of solid hearts with water and place an open-center heart on each. Bake for 10–15 minutes. Remove baking sheet from oven. Remove cookies from sheet. Let cool. Pat together remaining dough. Place on clean buttered and floured baking sheet. Repeat steps 4–6.

CONES

Ingredients (for about 6–8 cones)
- cookie dough (page 25)
- whipped cream
- multicolored sprinkles

1 While dough is chilling for 1 hour, prepare the paper cones. Cut about 8 3-x-5-inch paper rectangles. Roll each into a cone, moistening the tip to hold it together. Preheat the oven to 350° F.

2

Using strainer, sprinkle confectioners' sugar over each cookie. Melt one of the jams in the saucepan over low heat. Carefully spoon it into half the hollowed-out heart shapes. Melt the other jam and repeat for remaining hearts.

Roll out half the dough on a buttered and floured baking sheet and cut into 8-x-1-inch strips. Brush strips lightly with water. Place a paper cone on the end of one strip and roll the dough around the cone. Repeat for each strip.

TIP:
The cones can also be filled with vanilla or chocolate custard (page 43). Don't fill cones until just before serving or they will soften.

Remove any excess dough and bake cones for 15–20 minutes. Remove baking sheet from oven with pot holder. Using spatula, put cookies on a rack to cool. Repeat steps for remaining dough. When cool, remove the paper cones and fill each cookie with whipped cream. Top with sprinkles.

FLOWER COOKIES

Ingredients (for about 6–8 cookies)
- cookie dough (page 25)
Fillings of choice:
- whipped cream
- chopped fresh fruit: kiwis, strawberries, or other
- different kinds of jam
- melted semisweet chocolate
- multicolored sprinkles

Chill the dough for 1 hour. Preheat the oven to 350° F. Roll out half the dough on a buttered and floured baking sheet and cut with a 3-inch scalloped round cutter. Make small balls out of aluminum foil. Put these balls on the baking sheet and mold one cookie over each. Remove excess dough and set aside. Bake for 15–20 minutes. Take baking sheet out of oven with pot holder. Let the cookies cool on the sheet. Turn over the cookies and remove the foil balls. Repeat with remaining dough. Fill cookies with whipped cream, jam, or melted chocolate, and top with fruit or sprinkles.

MOONS AND STARS

Ingredients (for about 8–10 cookies)
- cookie dough (page 25)
- 1 tablespoon cocoa powder

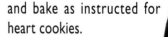

Prepare step 1 of plain cookie dough then divide the mixture in half. Add half the flour to one batch. Mix well. Stir cocoa into remaining flour and add to the other batch. Chill for 1 hour. Preheat the oven to 350° F. Roll out, cut shapes, assemble, and bake as instructed for heart cookies.

The cookie dough used here is of French origin. It is the basis for numerous pastry dishes, from simple cookies and tarts to elaborate pastry creations. In France it is called *pâte sablée*, or "sand pastry," because it makes a crumbly, "sandy" shortbread cookie.

Ragueneau in *Cyrano de Bergerac* reciting his recipe for almond tarts. Lafitte, 1910.

SUGAR

For many years refined white sugar was worth its weight in silver. Sugar is made from the juice of a giant grass called "sugar cane." Although people have known about sugar cane's sweet juice for more than ten thousand years, white sugar has been rare until modern times, because it was difficult to make. The juice must be squeezed out of the plant, cleaned, and dried so it will form crystals. Even then, the sugar is dark brown because of the molasses it contains, and further processing is needed. Sugar has been used in a number of ways apart from sweetening. It was a medicine, a seasoning for food, and a food preservative. One doctor even recommended it as toothpaste! Sugar was also a status symbol. The rich merchants of Venice, Italy, who controlled the sugar trade from the Orient, served a visiting king a meal at which everything on the table was made of spun sugar, including the bread, dishes, deocrations, tablecloth and napkins, and knives and forks!

ALMOND TARTS

Almond tarts are a popular pastry in France. They were invented by Cyprien Ragueneau, a seventeenth-century pastry chef. Although making pastry was his occupation, he loved poetry more than anything else. He would cook for poets and let them pay him with poems instead of money, so he died very poor. He is, however, the only pastry chef to appear as a character in a play. In the famous play *Cyrano de Bergerac*, by Edmond Rostand, the character Ragueneau recites as a poem his whole recipe for almond tarts.

PETITS FOURS

These pastries were named in eighteenth-century France, where they were baked á *petit feu* (on a small fire). In the United States, the name refers to tiny cakes covered with icing. In France, many small baked goods are called petits fours, including tiny cheese tarts served as appetizers, miniature eclairs, candied fruits, and some cookies.

The French translate chocolate chip cookie as "petit four of the toll house."

Lithograph. Petits Fours *from Large to Small.*

DESSERT BEFORE DINNER

Until the early 1800s, dessert was not a separate course at the end of the meal. People ate sweet dishes during the meal or between courses. Even after dessert had its modern place on the menu, poor families in England often ate a sweet "pudding" before the main course at dinner. The pudding (of flour, beef fat, and sugar or jam) was cheap to make, and "spoiled" the family's appetite before the more expensive parts of the meal were served.

THE WEDDING CAKE

The wedding cake is an important part of most marriage receptions. The bride and groom select their cake carefully, and it occupies a place of honor throughout the wedding meal. There are a number of traditions about wedding cake. At the end of the meal, the bride cuts the cake and feeds the first piece to the groom. They then offer a piece to each guest. In some countries, the remaining cake is cut and sent by mail in elegant boxes to guests who were not able to attend the wedding. Also, tradition says that if an unmarried girl places a piece of wedding cake under her pillow, she will dream of her future husband.

A large grocery store in England. Anonymous painting, about 1900.

31

TART TATIN

Utensils
- mixing bowls
- 10-inch pie pan
- large frying pan
- measuring cup
- pot holder
- wooden spoon
- glass tumbler
- tablespoon and fork
- pastry brush
- knife
- vegetable peeler
- kitchen scissors
- rolling pin
- plastic wrap

Ingredients
- 1 3/4 cups all-purpose flour
- 1 large egg, lightly beaten
- pinch of salt
- 10 tablespoons (1 1/4 sticks) unsalted butter,
  at room temperature
- 1/2 cup water
- 2 pounds tart apples
- 6 tablespoons sugar

Put the flour in a large bowl and make a well in the center. Add the egg, salt, and 7 tablespoons of butter cut into small pieces. Work the dough lightly with the fingertips until well mixed, then gradually add a few spoonfuls of water to hold the ingredients together. The dough should be firm. Gather it into a ball, wrap in plastic, and chill in the refrigerator for at least 1 hour.

1

Preheat the oven to 400° F. Peel and quarter the apples, then remove the cores. Sauté the apples in 2 tablespoons butter until golden, but not soft (about 3 minutes).

SAUTÉ:
to cook quickly in an open pan in a small amount of oil.

2

3

Layer the bottom of the pie pan with 2 table-spoons of sugar. Dot it with a few pieces of butter.

TIP:
Tart Tatin is good with vanilla ice cream.

4

Line the pie pan with the apples. Sprinkle the remaining sugar over the apples and dot with remaining butter.

5 Remove dough from refrigerator. It will be quite hard. Place dough on a floured surface and roll out until it is a little bigger than the pie pan. Cover apples with dough, then cut around the edge of the

pie pan with scissors to remove excess dough. Press dough all around the edge of the pie pan with a fork, and prick holes in the dough. Bake for 30 minutes, or until crust is golden.

Remove tart from oven with pot holder. Let it cool for about 15 minutes, or until pan is cool enough to hold. Place a serving plate upside down over the tart. Hold tightly onto both plate and pie pan, and turn the tart over onto the plate. The juice may leak, so work over the sink.

MIXED FRUIT TART

Ingredients
- pie dough (page 33)
- 1 egg yolk, slightly beaten
- fresh fruit: raspberries, currants, sliced kiwis
- vanilla custard (page 43)

Let the pie crust cool, then spoon a thin layer of custard into each section. Fill each section with fruit as shown.

TIP:
Tarts can be made of whatever fruits are in season as long as they are not overly juicy.

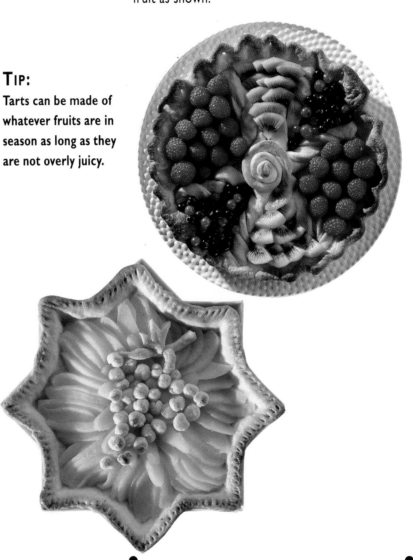

Chill pie dough as instructed on page 34. Preheat oven to 450° F. Set aside a small amount of dough for twists. Roll out dough on a floured surface and line pie pan, leaving about 1/2 inch hanging over the side. Roll out remaining dough and cut 13 strips about 1/2 inch wide. Twist 2 strips together and place on the bottom of the pan, moistening it slightly with water so it will stick. Make 5 more twists and arrange them in pan as shown. Wind remaining strip of dough into a flower and place in center of pan. Prick dough on the bottom of the pan with fork. Brush with beaten egg yoke. Crimp edge with fork. Bake for 30 minutes.

Leftover dough can be made into pastry decorations such as the bunch of grapes shown above. Tarts can be baked in pans of different shapes, too.

CHOCOLATE AND PEAR TART

Ingredients
- pie dough (page 33)
- 4 ounces (4 squares) semisweet chocolate, broken into pieces
- 2 cups canned pears halves, drained
- 1 large egg
- 1 tablespoon heavy cream
- 1/4 teaspoon vanilla extract

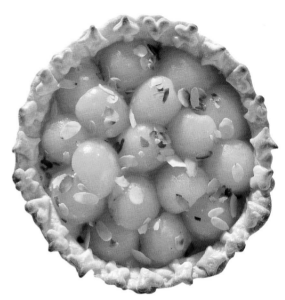

TIP:
The pear tart is good hot or cold. Sprinkle the top with sweetened cocoa powder.

Chill the pie dough as instructed on page 34. Preheat oven to 450° F. Roll out the dough and line a pie pan, leaving 1/2 inch hanging over the side. Melt chocolate in a double boiler. Pour it into the bottom of the tart and spread it evenly with a spatula.

Dry pears with a paper towel. Cut each pear into thin lengthwise slices, leaving one end uncut. Place them on the chocolate. Press down lightly, and they will open like a fan. In a bowl beat the egg, cream, and vanilla. Pour this mixture over the pears. Crimp edge with fork. Bake for 35 minutes.

DOUBLE BOILER
This consists of a smaller saucepan resting inside a larger saucepan. Food in the upper pan is heated slowly by the hot water in the lower one.

DECORATED TART

Ingredients
- pie dough (page 33)
- 1 large egg yolk, slightly beaten
- vanilla custard (page 43)
- 2 cups canned apricots halves, drained
- 3/4 cup sliced almonds

Chill the pie dough as instructed on page 34. Preheat the oven to 400° F. Line a pie pan, cutting off any excess dough. Make the remaining dough into a ball and roll it out again. Cut out various shapes with small cookie cutters. Use a pastry brush dipped in water to moisten the edge of the dough in the pan, and attach the shapes. Brush the decorated edge with egg yolk. Bake for 25 minutes. Let the crust cool, then spoon a thin layer of custard into it. Arrange the apricots on the custard. Toast the almonds in a frying pan over low heat, then sprinkle over the apricots.

This pie dough *(pâte brisée)* is the classic shell for tarts and pies, but it is also used as a crust to surround pâtés and to cover meat pies.

Various shapes of sweet and savory pastry shells, as shown in *The Pastry Book*, by Jules Gouffé, 1873.

Desserts are not part of traditional Japanese meals, although the Japanese do eat rice-flour cookies with tea. These cookies are always formed into decorative shapes such as flowers or animals.

PIES AND TARTS

Some people say that a pie has an upper crust and a lower crust, while a tart has just a lower crust. But is a lemon meringue pie really a lemon meringue tart?

People have been making pies and tarts for more than eight hundred years, and have been putting toppings on some sort of crust for thousands. The first pies and tarts were not sweet. Pies in medieval times contained meat, poultry, or fish mixed with other ingredients. At banquets during the Middle Ages, some unusual fillings were used—live birds, for instance. The nursery song lines, "Four-and-twenty blackbirds baked in a pie / When the pie was opened, the birds began to sing" refer to a real dish. The song is wrong about one thing, though; the singing birds had not been baked. They were placed inside cooked crusts. Pies like that one were not meant to be eaten, of course. They were part of the entertainment.

No one is sure about the origin of the word *pie*. It is possible that it comes from the Latin word for magpie—a reference to that bird's habit of filling its nest with odd assortments of objects, just as a pie crust can be filled with a mixture of ingredients.

FIXED-HANDLE WOODEN ROLLING PIN

WOODEN ROLLING PIN WITH TURNING HANDLES

UPSIDE-DOWN TART

Tart Tatin is named after the Tatin sisters who ran a hotel and restaurant in a small town near Orléans, France. They became famous when they added this delicious tart to their menu. They didn't create it, though. The upside-down tart was a well-known local recipe often part of people's Sunday meals.

AS AMERICAN AS APPLE PIE?

Apple pie is a much-loved dessert in the United States, but the dish is much older than the country. The French, Italians, and English have served apple pie for centuries.

RIBBED ROLLING PIN

GLAZED GLASS ROLLING PIN

MULTICOLORED GLASS ROLLING PIN

ROLLING PIN WITH DESIGN

CAKES IN STORIES

Cakes and other sweet dishes are often important elements in stories. They can be rewards or they can be traps. Here are a few examples:

The Story of the Nutcracker
by E. T. A. Hoffmann
At Christmas, Clara receives a nutcracker doll, and at midnight he and all the other toys come to life. When Clara helps save the Nutcracker from his enemy, the King of the Rats, he rewards her by bringing her to the land of sweets.

Hansel and Gretel
by Jacob Grimm
The witch had no trouble attracting the two lost children to her house because the walls were made of gingerbread, the roof of cake, and the windows of spun sugar. Sweet things are no reward in this story!

The Story of Prince Casse Noisette (Prince Nutcracker), by Hoffmann. Illustration by C. Offterdinger. Paris, 1883.

Alice in Wonderland
by Lewis Carroll
Alice goes into a rabbit hole, falls down a well, and then discovers a tiny door. She drinks a potion and suddenly shrinks. Unfortunately, the key to the door is on a table far above her head. Looking around she finds a small cake marked "Eat me!" Alice does eat it, and then shoots up, growing larger than she was before. And thus begins Alice's adventures in Wonderland.

PARIS-BREST

Utensils
- medium saucepan
- whisk
- large mixing bowl
- wooden spoon
- tablespoon
- pencil
- 6-inch bowl
- kitchen scissors
- syringe, cookie press, or pastry bag with 1-inch
  star-shaped tube
- waxed or parchment paper
- pot holder
- large baking sheet
- sharp knife

Ingredients
- 1 cup milk
- 5 tablespoons unsalted butter, cut into pieces
- 1/2 teaspoon salt
- 1 1/4 cups all-purpose flour
- 1 tablespoon sugar
- 4 large eggs
- 1/2 cup sliced almonds
- chocolate custard (page 43)

Preheat the oven to 400° F. Put the milk, butter, and salt in the saucepan. Over low heat, stir mixture with the whisk until it just comes to a boil.

2

Remove the pan from the heat, and add the flour and sugar all at once. Mix thoroughly with the wooden spoon.

3

Break eggs into batter one at a time. Mix in each egg thoroughly before adding the next. Dough will get slippery.

4

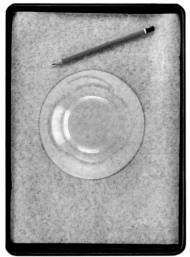

Cut a piece of paper to the size of the baking sheet. Turn the 6-inch bowl upside down on the paper and trace a circle around the edge. Remove the bowl.

TIP:
Never open the oven while pastry is baking. The pastry might not puff up.

6

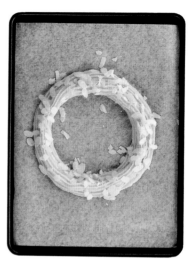

Sprinkle almonds over the ring. Bake for 25 minutes or until puffed and lightly browned. Remove baking sheet from oven with the pot holder. Let the pastry cool. Wash out syringe or pastry bag.

5

Fill the syringe or pastry bag with the batter. Draw a circle of batter on the pencil mark. Make a second circle inside the first—the two circles must be touching. Add a third ring on top of the bottom one.

7

Cut the pastry horizontally with a knife and scoop out some soft dough inside. Put the chocolate custard in the syringe or pastry bag and fill the bottom half of the ring with it. Replace the top half.

CHOCOLATE CUSTARD

Ingredients (for about 3 cups)
- 2 cups plus 2 tablespoons milk
- pinch of salt
- 3 ounces (3 squares) semisweet chocolate, broken into pieces
- 4 large egg yolks
- 3/4 cup sugar
- 1/4 cup all-purpose flour
- 5 tablespoons unsalted butter, at room temperature

TIP:
Lay plastic wrap directly on surface of custard to prevent a skin from forming.

2

In a bowl, beat the egg yolks and sugar with a whisk until the mixture turns very pale yellow. Beat in the flour. Add remaining 2 tablespoons of milk and mix well to avoid lumps. Gradually add the chocolate milk, stirring constantly. Pour this mixture into a saucepan and bring almost to a boil over a low heat, stirring constantly with the whisk to prevent sticking or burning. Remove the mixture from the heat and let cool. Add the softened butter when the custard is lukewarm and mix well. Chill in the refrigerator for 1 hour.

Put 2 cups of milk and the salt in a saucepan and bring to a boil over low heat. Remove pan from heat. Add the chocolate to the hot milk. Stir with whisk until chocolate is completely melted.

Vanilla custard
Leave out the chocolate from recipe and instead stir in 1 teaspoon vanilla extract when custard is lukewarm.

Éclairs and Cream Puffs

Ingredients
- cream puff batter (page 41)
- chocolate custard (page 43)
- 4 ounces (4 squares) semisweet chocolate
- colored sprinkles, silver candy balls (optional)

Preheat the oven to 400° F. Use syringe or attach a 1-inch tube to a pastry bag and fill with batter. For the éclairs, draw 3-inch lengths on a buttered and floured baking sheet; for cream puffs, shape 1-inch balls. Bake for 15 minutes or until puffed and lightly browned. Remove the pastries from the oven cool on a rack.

Cut the éclairs or puffs along one side and fill with the custard. For the icing, melt the chocolate in a double boiler and spread over the éclairs and cream puffs with a spatula. Decorate with sprinkles or silver candy balls if desired.

IMPORTANT:
Large and small pastries for Pierrot must be baked separately. If the oven is opened while cream puff pastry is baking, it may fail to puff up.

Pierrot (the clown)

Ingredients
- cream puff batter (page 41)
- vanilla and chocolate custard (page 43)
- 3 ounces (3 squares) semisweet chocolate
- royal icing (page 49)
- red, green, and yellow food coloring
- candied almonds
- icing flowers
- 2 gum drops or other candies

Preheat the oven to 400° F. To make the head, shape a ball of batter the size of an orange in the middle of a buttered and floured baking sheet. Bake for 25 minutes, or until puffed and lightly browned. Remove from oven, but leave oven on. Let pastry cool, then cut in half horizontally, scoop out inside, and fill with chocolate custard. To form the ruff, make about 15 walnut-size balls with the remaining batter. Bake at 400° F for 15 minutes, then cool. Cut open and fill with vanilla custard.

Melt chocolate in double boiler and ice the head. Put it on a large plate. Tint royal icing to desired shades. Attach the smaller pastries all around with icing. Place candied almonds and icing flowers between the small pastries, attaching pieces of candy with icing. Make the clown's eyes by attaching candies.

Cream puff pastry (*pâte á choux*) is one of two classic French pastries that puff up when baked. The other is puff pastry or *pâte feuilletée* (leaf pastry). Puff pastry consists of dough and butter that are rolled out and folded four or more times, until there are multiple paper-thin layers. The pastry rises in the oven as the air and moisture between the layers expand in the heat. It is delicious, but difficult to make.

Croquembouche—which means "crunches in the mouth"—is a towering dessert made of glazed cream puffs, almond and pistachios. From *The Pastry Book*, by Jules Gouffé, 1873.

THE PARIS-BREST

Bicycle racing became popular in France in the 1890s, when bicycling was a new outdoor activity. One famous race took place each year between Paris and Brest. A pastry chef whose shop was on the race route between the two cities had the idea of making éclairs shaped like bicycle wheels. This innovation attracted numerous customers and the dessert is still served in France today.

Le Petit Journal
SUPPLÉMENT ILLUSTRÉ
Le Petit Journal
CHAQUE JOUR 5 CENTIMES
Le Supplément illustré
CHAQUE SEMAINE 5 CENTIMES
Huit pages : CINQ centimes
ABONNEMENTS

DIMANCHE 1ᵉʳ SEPTEMBRE 1901   Numéro 563

MAURICE GARIN
Vainqueur de la course Paris-Brest

OVENS

In early times, an oven was nothing more than a hole in the ground. People cooked food by covering it with hot rocks or ashes. Later, oval or round ovens were constructed from clay, rocks, or bricks. Some of these were heated by a fire set inside. The cook removed the fire before putting the food in. During the Middle Ages, the oven was often in the center of a village and everyone had a turn using it. By the eighteenth century, the oven had developed into the stove, used for both baking and heating the home. Still fueled by coal or wood, the stove temperature was regulated only by adjusting the intensity of the fire. An experienced cook knew how to test the oven's temperature; one way was to put a hand into the hot oven and count the time until the heat became unbearable. By the late nineteenth century, gas and electric stoves with adjustable temperatures made cooking and baking much easier.

HOW DO PASTRIES GET THEIR NAMES?

A pastry might be named after its inventor, the place it was created, or something it resembles. Or it can be named in someone's honor. In England, for example, desserts are often named for royalty.
The panetone (an Italian coffee cake) owes its name to a contraction of *pane de Tonio* (bread of Tony). Tony was a poor baker in Milan. A young nobleman had fallen in love with his daughter, but marriage was impossible because the baker could not provide a dowry—the money a bride's father traditionally gave the groom. The baker worked desperately to invent a new creation that would bring him success. It was a triumph: the baker became rich and his daughter could marry.

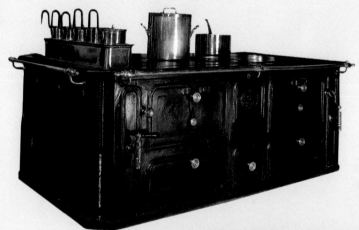

Cast-iron stove designed by Viollet-le-Duc, nineteenth century.

Ceramic mold for kugelhopf, a traditional French cake.

Baba au rhum is a variation of the kugelhopf. Stanislas Leczinski (see page 14) felt that the kugelhopf was too dry, so he soaked it in a rum-flavored syrup. Leczinski, who was reading *A Thousand and One Nights* at the time, named this discovery after the book's hero, Ali Baba.

CAKE HOUSE

Utensils
- cooling rack
- 7 x 9-inch cake pan
- serrated knife
- plastic spatula
- electric hand mixer
- wooden spoon
- strainer
- tablespoon
- long metal spatula
- 2 pot holders
- large and small mixing bowls
- whisk
- small and medium saucepans

Ingredients

For the cake
- 6 large eggs
- 3/4 cup granulated sugar
- pinch of salt
- 1 teaspoon baking powder
- 1 1/2 cups all-purpose flour
- 4 tablespoons (1/2 stick) unsalted butter

For the royal icing
- 1 1/2 cups sifted confectioners' sugar
- 1 large egg white
- several drops of lemon juice

For decoration
- multicolored sprinkles
- chocolate sprinkles
- small candies
- plain cookies, such as vanilla wafers
- thin chocolate cookies

TIP:
Bake the cake the day before it is to be decorated and served. It will taste better and be easier to cut.

1

Preheat the oven to 350° F. Break the eggs into the large bowl. Add the granulated sugar and salt. Place the bowl in a saucepan containing hot (not boiling) water and place saucepan over low heat. Mix thoroughly with whisk, until foamy and warm.

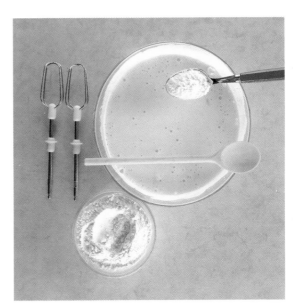

2 Remove bowl from pan and beat with electric mixer until mixture triples in volume and becomes very light yellow. It should be warm but not hot. Mix baking powder into flour. Very gradually add flour mixture, folding gently with wooden spoon.

3

Melt the butter over low heat, then fold gently into the batter using the plastic spatula. The batter should remain light; do not overmix. Pour the batter into the buttered and floured cake pan.

TIP:
To "fold in" means to sprinkle a small amount of an ingredient on top of the batter and lift and fold the batter around it. This gentle motion helps keep the air bubbles trapped in the batter, to help the cake rise.

4

Bake for 30–35 minutes, or until golden. To test if the cake is done, insert a toothpick in the center. If it comes out clean, the cake is ready to be removed from the oven.

5

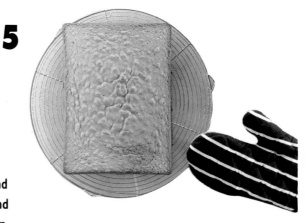

Take the cake out of the oven. Let cool 3 minutes, then place a cooling rack upside down on top of the cake. Using 2 pot holders, turn the pan over quickly. Let it cool completely on the rack. If the cake sticks to the pan, slide a plastic spatula around the edges of the cake.

6

For royal icing, use the electric mixer to beat together confectioners' sugar, egg white, and lemon juice. The icing must be smooth and white.

BERRY LAYER CAKE

Ingredients
- 1 baked 7 x 9-inch yellow cake (page 49)
- 2 different fruit jellies or jams
- 1 1/4 cups sifted confectioners' sugar
- 2 tablespoons water
- 2 or 3 kinds of fresh berries: raspberries, blackberries, strawberries, or currants

TIP:
When using royal icing, work quickly because it becomes hard soon after it is made. Keep it covered when not in use.

Using a serrated knife, cut 2 corners off the cake to form a peaked roof. With the metal spatula, spread icing over the top of the cake. Decorate with cookies and candies to look like a house. Use photograph for ideas.

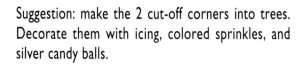

Suggestion: make the 2 cut-off corners into trees. Decorate them with icing, colored sprinkles, and silver candy balls.

Using a serrated knife, cut the cake into an 8-inch square. Carefully cut it horizontally into 3 equal layers. Cover the first layer with one kind of jelly. Place the second layer on top and spread it with the second kind of jelly. Place last layer of cake on top.

To make the glaze, put the confectioners' sugar in the top of a double boiler. Gradually add the water. Heat, mixing until it becomes smooth. Remove double boiler from heat. Pour glaze over center of cake, letting it drip down the sides. With a spatula, spread it evenly over the top. Arrange fruits on top in a pattern. Refrigerate for 30 minutes before serving.

STRAWBERRY CAKE

Ingredients
- 1 baked 10-inch round yellow cake (page 49)
- 1 pint strawberries
- whipped cream
- sifted confectioners' sugar

Place an 8-inch plate over the cake and cut all around the edge.

Wash the strawberries and remove their hulls. Set aside a few whole berries for decoration, and cut the rest into small pieces.

Keeping the cake flat, cut it in half horizontally with the serrated knife. Cover the bottom layer with whipped cream and arrange the strawberry pieces on it. Place the second layer on top.

Place a paper doily on top of the cake and dust with confectioners' sugar. Remove the paper carefully and decorate cake with remaining strawberries cut into halves or quarters.

CHOCOLATE CAKE

Ingredients
- cake batter (page 49)
- 1/3 cup unsweetened cocoa powder
- 8 ounces (8 squares) semisweet chocolate
- chocolate decorations (semisweet chocolate bits, sprinkles, chocolate-covered coffee beans)

Prepare the batter as instructed on pages 49–50, but add the cocoa along with the flour, mixing with a wooden spoon. Bake in 10-inch round pan. After the cake has cooled, break the chocolate into small pieces and melt in a double boiler. Pour the chocolate glaze over the center of the baked cake, letting it drip down the sides. Spread the glaze evenly over the top with a spatula. Decorate the cake with chocolate bits, sprinkles, or coffee beans.

The type of cake used in these recipes is the genoise, named for the town of Genoa, in northern Italy. Leavening a cake with beaten egg yolks is a technique any experienced French or Italian baker knows. In the United States, bakers leaven yellow cakes with baking powder. But both types of yellow cake are the basis for many other kinds of cake, such as birthday cakes, layer cakes, Baked Alaska, or, when cut into small pieces, iced petits fours.

THE ART OF PASTRY

Mixing flour with other ingredients to make dough is older than recorded history, but the techniques changed greatly after the Crusaders returned to Europe with methods and ingredients from the East. Working with dough became an art. In France, these craftspeople were called *oublieurs*. The name came from a kind of flat waffle or wafer known as *oublies*, which is still eaten today.

In 1440 the king of France decided to grant pastry chefs the exclusive right to make meat and fish pies and sweet cakes. Bakers were allowed to make only bread. Eventually other professions took over the making of pies that were not sweet, and bread and pastry making again became one profession. Nevertheless, in France people often buy bread in a bread shop and fine pastries in a pastry shop.

A traditional English Christmas pudding decorated with holly.

Christmas pudding in England is often called plum pudding, but it does not have any plums in it. Decades ago, all dried fruits were called plums because many of them look like dried plums, or prunes. The "plums" in a Christmas pudding are often raisins or currants.

ANTOINE CARÊME

Antoine Carême was one of the greatest cooks and pastry chefs in history. Born in 1783, of a poor family, he was forced to leave home and earn a living when he was only ten years old. He found work in the kitchen of a shop that sold cooked food, and there he began his long career. Talented and hard-working, Carême was quickly noticed by the minister Talleyrand, an important political figure of the time. He was employed by the kings and queens of several countries and was able to learn from the cooking traditions of each country. He adapted them to French tastes, influencing foreign cuisine at the same time.

Carême wrote many books on cooking and pastry making. He was one of the first people to write recipes so clearly that less experienced cooks could follow them, and many of the recipes he invented are still in use today wherever French food is cooked.

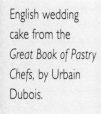

English wedding cake from the *Great Book of Pastry Chefs*, by Urbain Dubois.

Portrait of Antoine Carême.

Carême was particularly famous for his pastry and for elaborate constructions made of sugar. Fancy sugar and pastry sculptures were popular in Europe from the Renaissance through the earlier part of the twentieth century. Carême produced hundreds of designs for spun-sugar castles, forts, ruins, and other buildings. Some of these were meant as decoration; some were to be eaten.

Wedding cakes, which often have columns supporting the layers and complicated decorations made of sugar, are among the modern-day descendants of the sugar sculptures and highly decorated desserts that Carême loved to design and build.

INDEX OF RECIPES

First American edition 1994 published by Ticknor & Fields Books for Young Readers, A Houghton Mifflin company, 215 Park Avenue South, New York, New York 10003. • Copyright © by Hachette, Paris, 1992 • English translation copyright © 1994 by Ticknor & Fields Books for Young Readers • First published in France by Hachette • All rights reserved. • For information about permission to reproduce selections from this book, write to Permissions, Ticknor & Fields, 215 Park Avenue South, New York, New York 10003. • Manufactured in France • The text of this book is set in 13 point Gill Sans

10 9 8 7 6 5 4 3 2 1

Photo credits: • © Edimédia, pages 14, 38, 46, 47 • © Roger Guillemot / Edimédia, page 47 • © Jean-Loup Charmet, pages 15, 31, 39, 54 • © Bedfordshire, pages 38, 39 • © Photothèque Perrin, page 30 • © Kharbine / Tapabor, pages 23, 31 • © FPG International / Explorer, page 22 • © Mary Evans Picture Library / Explorer, page 23, 55

Library of Congress Cataloging-in-Publication Data

Rosin, Arielle.
    Éclairs & brown bears / by Arielle Rosin; photographs by Daniel Czap; research by Etienne Collomb. — 1st American ed.
        p.   cm. — (Young gourmet)
    Includes index.
    Summary: Step-by-step introduction to the baking of desserts such as bear-shaped meringues dipped in chocolate and brownies with M&Ms. Also includes historical background relating to the foods.
    ISBN 0-395-68380-7
    1. Pastry—Juvenile literature. 2. Cake—Juvenile literature. [1. Baking. 2. Desserts. 3. Cookery.] I. Czap, Daniel, ill. II. Title. III. Title: Éclairs & brown bears. IV. Series.
TX773.R79313 1994
641.8'65—dc20   93-24971   CIP   AC

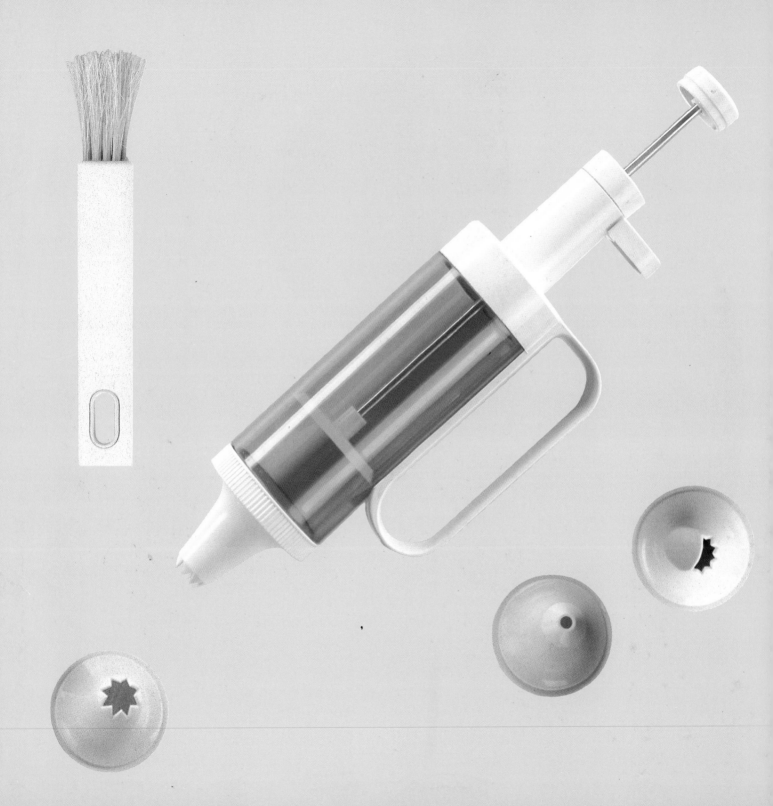